Good breeding can show itself in
good taste, good manners and good cooking.

These traditional recipes were used
in days gone by in the very best households.

RECIPES
for
HIGH CLASS
COOKERY

Copper Beech Publishing

Published in Great Britain by
Copper Beech Publishing Ltd
© Copper Beech Publishing Ltd 2001

Editor Julie Lessels

ISBN 978-1-898617-30-3

A CIP catalogue record for this book is available from the
British Library.

Copper Beech Publishing Ltd
P O Box 159 East Grinstead
Sussex England RH19 4FS

STOCK &
SOUP

In every household a stock-pot should be in general use. In large houses where much cooking is done, it is better to have one fitted with a tap.

Nothing must be added to a stock-pot unless it is clean and contains some goodness.

*B*rown Stock

Ingredients
2 lbs shin or shoulder of beef
1 small carrot   1 small onion
½ teaspoonful salt   2 quarts cold water
10 small peppercorns
½ teaspoonful celery seeds tied in muslin

Method: Measure the water into a strong pan; add salt. Wipe and cut the meat into small pieces and add to the water. Scrape the bone well, remove the marrow, wash to remove the fat, and add to the pan. Bring the stock slowly to boiling-point; this will take about three-quarters of an hour. Remove any scum; add the prepared vegetables cut into large pieces. Simmer for three to four hours. Strain through a hair sieve. When cold, skim thoroughly. The stock is then ready for soups &c.

For white stock, use knuckle of veal or bones and trimmings of chickens instead of beef. White stock omits the carrot.

*F*ish Stock

Ingredients

Twopennyworth of fish trimmings
1 onion   1 stick of celery   1 blade of mace
6 white peppercorns   1 quart cold water
Salt to taste

Method: Thoroughly cleanse the trimmings, and put them into a saucepan with the water and salt. Bring slowly to the boil, and skim thoroughly; add peppercorns, celery and mace, and allow all to simmer for forty minutes, then strain. This stock can be used for fish soup or sauce.

If fish stock is cooked too long a bitter flavour is extracted from the bones.

Consommé

Ingredients

To clear 1 quart of stock:

1 small piece of carrot   1 small piece of onion
¼ lb lean juicy beef   1 white and shell of egg
1 blade of mace   6 peppercorns   salt

Method: The stock should be cold for clarifying. Remove all fat, shred the lean beef, and soak it for fifteen minutes in one gill of water. Prepare the vegetables, and cut in slices. Put all the ingredients into a clean rinsed pan, and whisk over a clear fire until almost at boiling-point. Remove the whisk, and allow the stock to boil up with force; then let it infuse for thirty minutes, and strain through a dry cloth. The consommé is then ready for reheating, and may be garnished according to taste. A little light sherry may be added if desired.

All garnishes should be rinsed if possible.

Consommé à la Jardiniere

Ingredients

1 quart clear stock

Garnish ~ 1 tablespoonful turnip in pea shapes

1 tablespoonful carrot in pea shapes

1 tablespoonful green peas

1 tablespoonful cauliflower sprigs

Method: Cut out of the carrot and turnip round pieces the shape of peas, using a special vegetable cutter for the purpose. Use the red part only of the carrot. Cut the pieces of cauliflower in small sprigs. Cook the vegetables in separate pans of boiling salted water until tender, then drain. Put the clear stock into a saucepan, and bring to the boil. Add the garnish of vegetables, and the consommé is ready for serving.

The table glass should always be of as good a quality as possible, and the design should be characterised by its refined simplicity.

*C*lear Mulligatawny

Ingredients

1 quart stock   4oz juicy beef   1 gill water
1 white and shell of egg   1 onion
1 tablespoonful curry powder
1 teaspoonful curry paste   1 small carrot
½ apple   salt and lemon juice to taste
Garnish ~ 2oz cooked chicken

Method: Shred the beef, and mix it with the water; add to it the curry powder and paste; soak for fifteen minutes. Put all ingredients into a clean saucepan. Whisk till almost boiling. Simmer for thirty minutes, and strain. Reheat; add the chicken cut in dice, and serve with rice.

Tomato Soup

Ingredients

1 lb fresh tomatoes   1oz butter   1oz lean ham
1 small piece celery   1 small piece carrot
1 onion   1 bay leaf   6 peppercorns
1½ pints light-coloured stock or tomato liquor
¾ oz cornflour   ½ gill milk   1 gill cream
Salt to taste

Method: Melt the butter, fry the bacon and vegetables cut in slices; add the tomatoes, break them down, and boil quickly for five minutes. Add stock, peppercorns, and bay leaf. Simmer for one hour, and strain. Mix the cornflour with the milk, add to the soup, and boil for ten minutes. Add the cream and seasoning.

*B*isque of Lobster

Ingredients

½ lobster, cooked   1 quart fish stock
2oz butter   2oz rice-flour   1 onion   ½ carrot
1 bay leaf   1 sprig of parsley   ½ gill cream
1 teaspoonful anchovy essence
½ gill sherry   1oz butter
Cayenne pepper, salt, lemon juice

Method: Remove the meat from the lobster and reserve the best pieces. Wash and break half of the shell. Melt the butter, fry the onion, carrot, bay leaf, and parsley; add the rice-flour and the shell. Add the stock by degrees, and the broken pieces of lobster. Simmer for forty minutes, and strain through a hair sieve. Re-heat; add the anchovy essence, cream, and sherry. Whisk in the butter gradually without boiling, and add the remainder of the lobster cut in neat pieces.

I'LL WRITE THIS DOWN LEST I FORGET IT

One cannot be too careful when buying lobsters. But it is perfectly easy to get sound ones if you just keep one little point in mind. Always make sure that the tail is curled up tight to the body, and you will run no risk of getting anything but a lobster that was sound when cooked.

How to choose fish:
The body of the fish should be stiff and
the gills red. If not, it may be concluded
that the fish is not fresh.

Double Roasting-Tin.

FISH & ENTRÉES

The silver should be taken from the sideboard and everything must be carried to the table on a tray and never in the hands.

Sole Au Gratin

Ingredients

1 medium-sized sole
1 teaspoonful chopped parsley
1 teaspoonful chopped mushroom
1 teaspoonful chopped onion
½ cup breadcrumbs   a little melted butter
pepper, salt, and lemon juice
1 gill good brown sauce

Method: Wash, clean and skin the sole; trim the fins and tail, and score each side. Mix the parsley, mushroom and onion together; sprinkle half of it in a greased gratin dish. Season the fish and lay it in the dish white side up. Spread the remainder of the mixture on the top, scatter lightly with breadcrumbs and sprinkle over a little melted butter. Cook the sole in a moderately hot oven about thirty minutes. Pour the sauce round, and serve.

*B*oiled Turbot

Method: Clean the fish thoroughly and rub over with lemon. Have a pan of simmering salted water ready, add a little vinegar, and let the fish cook gently without boiling. Time ~ Ten minutes to each pound and ten minutes over. Drain thoroughly and serve on to a napkin and garnish with parsley and lemon. Serve with any good fish sauce, hot or cold.

Please note ~ all fish is boiled in the same manner with the exception of salmon, when the acids are omitted.

*F*ish Soufflé

Ingredients

½ lb white fish   2oz flour   1oz butter
1 gill fish stock   3 eggs   ½ gill cream
Coating ~ ½ pint white fish sauce
Garnish ~ red pepper or parsley

Method: Make a sauce with the flour, butter and stock. Scrape fish from the bone; add the sauce, eggs, and seasonings, and rub through a wire sieve. Stir in the cream and turn into a plain mould, greased and dusted with rice-flour. Steam gently till firm, about one hour. Add coating, decorate to taste and serve.

*F*ried Whitebait

Method: Pick the whitebait and rinse quickly in cold water. Shake on a floured cloth to dry. Lay them loosely in a frying-basket and cook in hot fat. Plunge into a second pan of very hot fat to crisp them. Drain well, and dish on to a napkin. Garnish with lemon and fried parsley. Serve with thick brown bread and butter.

*S*avoury Lobster Cream

Ingredients

¼ lb cooked lobster
1 gill cream   ½ gill aspic   ½ gill tomato pulp
1 teaspoonful mayonnaise
Cayenne, salt, and lemon juice
¼ oz gelatine   ¼ gill water

Method: Line a border mould thinly with aspic, and decorate with neat claw pieces of lobster, truffle &c. Chop and pound the lobster. Whip the cream lightly, and mix all the ingredients together, adding the dissolved gelatine last and mould when beginning to thicken. Turn out when set, and decorate with mayonnaise, salad, lobster feelers, and chopped aspic jelly, as desired.

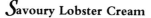

Please note ~ crayfish, shrimps &c. may be substituted for lobster. This savoury fish cream may also be moulded in small moulds.

Flowers to decorate the dinner table should be gathered early in the morning or late in the evening, never in the heat of the day; and before being arranged they should be put in roomy jars or basins of water and set aside in a shady and cool (but not icy-cold) place for at least a couple of hours. If cut at the joints they retain their freshness longer than if the incision is made at a point between them.

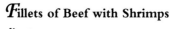Fillets of Beef with Shrimps

Ingredients

1½ lbs lean beef   2oz butter
¼ pint carefully picked shrimps
½ pint stock   1 teaspoonful flour
½ teaspoonful lemon juice salt and pepper

Method: Divide the meat into eight fillets, half an inch thick. Heat the butter in a heavy pan until brown, put in the fillets, fry quickly until brown on one side, turn and cook the underside. Lift out of the pan and keep hot. Pour away nearly all the butter, add the flour to the pan and heat. Add stock, boil and add seasoning, lemon juice and shrimps. Dish the fillets in a row, pour over the gravy and shrimps and garnish the dish with horseradish. Serve immediately.

*Have a damask cloth of the whitest
and finest that can be afforded.*

*M*utton Cutlets

Ingredients

5 bones of small mutton cutlets
1 beaten egg   Breadcrumbs
2 tablespoonfuls clarified fat
Dishing ~ potato border, ½ pint tomato sauce,
macedoine of vegetables

Method: Have the mutton well hung. Saw
the rib bones even in length, about three
inches, and remove the chine bone. Trim into
small neat cutlets, and scrape the bones clean.
Coat well with beaten egg and breadcrumbs.
Fry in smoking hot fat for seven to ten minutes,
then drain very thoroughly. Arrange the cutlets
on a border of potato, pour the sauce round,
and garnish with the vegetables.

*Please note ~ the potato border for dishing
is optional.*

*S*easonal Turkey Fillets

Ingredients

4 turkey breasts   1 small onion   2 eggs
Breadcrumbs   6 rashers bacon
Flour and butter to thicken
Pepper and salt to season
Butter or dripping for frying

Method: Put half a pint of boiling water in a stew-pan, season with pepper, salt, a pinch of herbs and the onion cut in slices. Cut the meat into small fillets, season, dip into beaten egg and breadcrumbs and fry in boiling fat till well-cooked. Dish up with the fried rashers of bacon made into neat little rolls. Make gravy and thicken with butter and flour. Boil up and pour round the turkey.

*T*imbales of Chicken

Ingredients

4oz cooked chicken   2oz cooked ham
1oz breadcrumbs 1 egg 1 gill white sauce
½ teaspoonful chopped truffle
1 teaspoonful cream, pepper and salt
1 teaspoonful each of
chopped parsley and chopped mushrooms
Garnish ~ cooked macaroni ½ pint tomato sauce

Method: Grease some small plain moulds and line with rings of cooked macaroni, or twists of spaghetti. Mince the chicken and ham, and mix all the ingredients together. Fill the moulds with this mixture. Steam till firm, twenty to thirty minutes. Turn out and pour the sauce round.

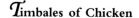

*When laying the table, the silver must be
placed evenly and about one inch up
from the edge of the table.*

Sweetbread à la Supreme

Ingredients

1 sweetbread ½ pint boiling stock
1 carrot 1 onion 1 stick celery
1 bunch herbs 1 blade of mace 6 peppercorns
Dishing ~ potato border, peas,
½ pint supreme sauce

Method: Prepare the sweetbread, put it in a stew-pan with the stock, vegetables, peppercorns, and mace; simmer it gently till quite tender, from one to one and a half hours. Dish the sweetbread onto the potato border, pour the supreme sauce over it and garnish with peas.

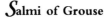

Salmi of Grouse

Ingredients

A brace of grouse   2oz butter   1oz flour
1 bayleaf   1 bunch of sweet herbs
1 onion   4 mushrooms freshly picked
1 small carrot   salt and pepper
1 glass of sherry   juice of 1 lemon
½ pint stock

Method: Prepare the grouse as usual and divide each bird into four pieces. Heat the butter and fry the grouse to a nice brown, lift out and fry the sliced carrot, onion and mushrooms. Then add the flour and heat gently, then add the stock, herbs, bayleaf, seasoning, and return the grouse to the pan. Simmer slowly, thirty to forty minutes. Lift out the grouse, strain the gravy into another pan, skim off the fat, add the sherry, lemon juice and mushrooms and reheat. Serve immediately.

Medallions of Chicken

Ingredients

2oz cooked chicken   ½oz cooked ham
½ gill cream   ½ gill aspic
2 chopped mushrooms
1 teaspoonful chopped truffle
pepper, salt, cayenne
6 rounds cooked ham
1½ gill Chaud-froid sauce
Decoration ~ cucumber, chervil &c.
6 slices tomato chopped aspic jelly

Method: Put the chicken and ham twice through a mincer and pound well. Add the mushrooms, truffle, seasonings and liquid aspic. Have the cream lightly beaten and stir in the chicken mixture. Put into medallion moulds. When set, turn out, and place each on a round of ham. Coat the medallions with the Chaud-froid sauce, decorate and glaze. Dish on slices of tomato, artichoke bottoms &c. Decorate with chopped aspic jelly.

The very best cooking will be spoiled if the dinner has to be kept back owing to the unpunctuality of some member of the family; while, on the other hand, the cook who cannot send up a dinner to time should remember that a meal that has to be waited for often fails to be appreciated.

BOILING-POT.

VEGETABLES

*The cooking of vegetables requires as much care
as the cooking of meat or the turning out of a
pudding, and the simplicity of the operation
should not be an excuse for slovenliness;
a vegetable must be tastefully seasoned,
well served and temptingly arranged.*

Artichokes

Ingredients

1 lb artichokes   ½ pint Béchamel sauce

Method: Wash, peel, and rinse the artichokes, having a little vinegar or lemon juice in each change of water to preserve the colour. Cook in boiling salted water, with a few drops of vinegar or lemon juice added, for thirty minutes. Drain, dish and coat with Béchamel sauce.

ARTICHOKES.

Asparagus

Ingredients

1 bunch asparagus   A little oiled butter
1 slice toast

Method: Trim the hard ends of the asparagus, scrape lightly, and tie up in bundles according to the thickness. Cook till tender in sufficient boiling salted water to just cover the asparagus, from twenty to thirty minutes. Drain, dish on the toast, and serve with oiled butter or mousseline sauce. An asparagus kettle should be used if possible.

Please note ~ too much water should be not be used for boiling delicately flavoured vegetables.

This delicacy from the garden will always delight and makes an impressive start to a really high class dinner.

Cauliflower Au Gratin

Ingredients

1 cauliflower   1oz butter   ½ oz flour
1 gill water   2oz Parmesan cheese
1 tablespoonful cream
Cayenne pepper and salt

Method: Trim, wash and boil the cauliflower. Drain it and put it on a fireproof dish. Make a thick sauce with the butter, flour, and water, add the seasonings, cream, and half of the cheese, and coat the cauliflower with it. Sprinkle the remainder of the cheese over, and brown in a hot oven.

Please note ~ Artichokes, parsnips, turnips, vegetable marrow, haricot beans &c. may be served in the same way.

*D*ressed French Beans

Ingredients

½ lb French beans   1oz butter
2 tablespoonfuls Velouté sauce
Lemon juice glaze, pepper and salt
Garnish ~ Fried bread, chopped parsley

Method: Wash and string the beans, and cut them into strips. Cook in boiling salted water till tender, about fifteen minutes, and drain thoroughly. Melt butter, add French beans, sauce, glaze and seasonings, and heat thoroughly. Pile in a vegetable dish, garnish with neat pieces of fried bread and a little chopped parsley.

Please note ~ the beans may be steamed instead of boiled, and may be tossed in a little melted butter.

Savoury Haricot Beans

Ingredients

½ lb haricot beans   1oz butter
1 yolk of egg   1oz cheddar cheese
1 dessertspoonful chopped parsley,
Cayenne, salt and a little cream

Method: Soak the beans overnight in plenty of cold water; rinse and put them in a pan with cold water and salt. Boil gently for two to three hours till tender. Drain, and remove the skins. Melt the butter in a pan; add all the other ingredients, and shake over the fire till the beans are well coated with the mixture, without allowing it to boil. Dish and garnish with fried bread.

COLANDER

When planning a menu, the colour and design of the dinner and dessert services should not be disregarded.

𝒫otato Croquettes

Ingredients

½ lb cooked potatoes   ½oz butter
1 yolk of egg   1 good teaspoonful parsley
1oz Parmesan cheese   Cayenne and salt

Method: Rub the potatoes through a sieve. Melt the butter in a pan; add the other ingredients, and cook over the fire till the mixture will roll smoothly into balls. Cool slightly, form into balls or fancy shapes; coat with beaten egg and breadcrumbs and fry in smoking hot fat. Drain well; dish and garnish with parsley.

Stuffed Tomatoes

Ingredients

3 medium firm tomatoes
Stuffing ~ 1 teaspoonful butter
½ teaspoonful chopped onion
1 dessertspoonful chopped ham
2 chopped button mushrooms
1 tablespoonful white breadcrumbs
A little brown sauce or tomato pulp
Cayenne and salt
Garnish for Top ~ Breadcrumbs and cheese
Dishing ~ Rounds of fried bread, parsley

Method: Have the tomatoes of equal sizes; wipe them and cut a small round from each at the end opposite the stalk. Scoop out all the pulp from the inside, and turn the cases upside down to drain. Melt the butter in a pan and fry the onion and ham thoroughly; stir in the other ingredients. Keep the mixture soft. Fill the tomatoes with this; sprinkle with cheese and crumbs on top, and bake in a moderate heat, for twelve to fifteen minutes. Dish on the rounds of fried bread and add sprigs of parsley.

Sweets are usually handed in the same way as entrées, a hot or cold plate with necessary fork or spoon and fork being put before each guest previously. In the case of any sweet requiring cutting, such as a tart, this should be served out in portions from the side.

HOT & COLD SWEETS

Baked soufflés are sent to the table in the tins in which they are baked and these are either slipped inside a hot silver case, or a warm serviette is folded round them. China dishes may be used instead of the tins if they are fireproof.

*A*lmond Tartlets

Ingredients

2oz almonds   1oz butter   1oz sugar   ½ egg
½ teaspoonful lemon juice
A little grated lemon rind   2oz shortcrust pastry

Method: Blanch the almonds and chop them finely. Cream the butter and sugar, and beat in the egg with the almonds, lemon juice, and rind. Make the pastry and roll it very thinly; cut in rounds, turn them, and line some greased patty tins evenly. Half fill the tins with the mixture. Put the tartlets in a hot oven till the pastry is set, then reduce the heat and cook the mixture more slowly. Cook for thirty to forty minutes, till firm and a pale brown colour.

In households where there are unexpected visitors, it is a good plan to keep some tartlet cases ready at hand. With some fresh fruit or preserve, they make a nice sweet in an emergency.

Chocolate Tartlets

Ingredients

½ stick (¾oz) chocolate   ½ gill milk
½ teaspoonful cornflour   ½ teaspoonful butter
1 teaspoonful sugar   1 yolk of egg
Vanilla essence   1 pinch of cinnamon
2oz shortcrust pastry
Meringue ~ 1 white of egg, 2oz sugar
Decoration ~ Cherries, angelica

Method: Dissolve the chocolate in half the milk, add the cornflour mixed with the remainder of the milk, and boil till thick. Cool, and stir in the rest of the ingredients. Line some greased tartlet tins with the pastry and half fill with the mixture. Place in a hot oven till the pastry is set and the mixture risen and firm, from twelve to fifteen minutes. Pipe the meringue on the top, dust with sugar, and decorate with the cherries and angelica cut in small pieces. Dry off in a very cool oven till crisp without browning, from three-quarters to one hour.

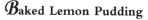

ℬaked Lemon Pudding

Ingredients

Puff pastry   3oz castor sugar
3 eggs   2 lemons   3oz cake-crumbs
½ gill milk

Method: Line and decorate the edges of a pie-dish with the pastry. Mix the yolks of eggs and the sugar well, then add the sieved cake-crumbs, the grated lemon rind, the strained lemon juice and the milk. Whip the whites of eggs stiffly and mix lightly with the other ingredients. Pour the mixture into the prepared pie-dish and bake in a moderate oven for about forty minutes.

*A*pple Charlotte

Ingredients

1½ lb apples   1oz butter   2 yolks of egg
2oz sugar   2 or 3 slices bread
Grated rind of a lemon   Juice of half a lemon
Clarified butter

Method: Peel, core, and slice the apples; put them in a pan with the butter, sugar, rind and juice of lemon and stew till soft. Rub this through a hair sieve, and add the yolks. Cut the bread into rounds the size of a shilling, and cut two large rounds to fit the top and bottom of the tin to be used. Dip the bread in the clarified butter, and place a large round at the foot of the tin. Arrange the small rounds in layers round the tin, lining it to the top. Fill the centre with the apple mixture, and place the other large round of bread on the top. Twist a greased paper over, place a saucer with a weight in it on the top, and bake in a hot oven for one hour. Turn on to a hot dish.

Plum Pudding

Ingredients

½ lb breadcrumbs   2oz flour   ½ lb suet
½ lb Valencias   ½ lb sultanas   ½ lb currants
2oz mixed peel   2oz citron peel   2oz almonds
½ lb demerara sugar   1 lemon   4 eggs
1 good teaspoonful mixed spices   1 gill brandy
1 gill rum (optional)   Milk if necessary
1 good pinch salt

Method: Chop the suet finely with the flour, stone the Valencias, clean and pick the currants and sultanas, chop the peel and almonds finely. Mix the breadcrumbs, suet, fruit, sugar, spices and salt, then add the lemon rind and juice. Beat the eggs and add to the mixture with the brandy and rum. Add milk if needed and have the mixture of a dropping consistency. Tie in floured cloths, or greased basins, and boil steadily, eight to twelve hours.

Please note ~ these puddings may be made several weeks before required, and should have two hours boiling at least when needed.

*V*anilla Soufflé

Ingredients

1oz butter   1oz flour   1 gill milk   1oz sugar
Vanilla essence   3 yolks of egg   4 whites of egg

Method: Tie a double band of paper round the outside of a soufflé tin and place a round of paper in the bottom. Grease thoroughly. Melt butter in a saucepan, stir in the flour, add the milk, and boil till the mixture is thick and leaves the sides of the pan clean. Cool slightly; add the sugar and beat in the yolks one by one; stir in the vanilla, a little of the beaten whites, then fold in the remainder as lightly as possible. Steam very gently till the soufflé is well risen and firm to the touch (three-quarters to one hour). Turn out and serve with jam or custard sauce.

A useful addition to any meal is a fruit salad. Almost any fruit may be employed as long as they are of the highest quality. The fruits must all be dry and perfectly ripe. All the cutting of the fruit must be done with a silver knife and a crystal salad bowl is the best to use to serve.

APRICOTS.

𝒫rune Tartlets with Claret

Ingredients

1 gill prune puree   ½ gill cream
A little claret, sugar, lemon juice
8 pastry cases
Decoration ~ 1 gill cream, pistachios &c.

Method: Mix the prune puree, cream, lemon juice, claret and sugar together. Fill the pastry cases with this mixture, and decorate with whipped cream, pistachios &c.

*A*pricot Cream

Ingredients

Wine jelly   Rounds of apricot   Pistachios
1 gill apricot puree   ½ gill apricot juice
1 gill double cream   Sugar and lemon juice
½oz gelatine   ½ gill water

Method: Decorate a mould with the jelly, apricot, and pistachios. Half-whip the cream; add the fruit puree and juice, sugar and lemon juice. Dissolve the gelatine in the water, and stir it gently into the mixture. Mould when beginning to thicken. Turn out when set, and garnish.

Please note ~ this method is employed in the making of all fruit creams.

Charlotte Russe

Ingredients

Sweet jelly   Pistachios   Cherries or violets
6 to 7 sponge finger biscuits   ½ pint cream
1 gill milk   Sugar   Vanilla   ½oz gelatine
5 drops lemon juice   ½ gill water

Method: Set some jelly in the foot of a plain charlotte tin and decorate to taste. Trim the biscuits evenly, and fit tightly round the sides of the tin. Half-whip the cream; stir in the milk, sugar, and flavourings, and add the dissolved gelatine. Leave till almost set, then pour into the tin. When set, trim the biscuits level with the cream; dip the bottom in water and turn out. Serve on a dish paper, or with chopped jelly round.

Please note ~ the bottom of the mould may be lined with biscuits instead of jelly, and decorated with whipped cream when turned out. Any cream filling may be substituted for the above mixture and the charlotte named accordingly.

Meringues

Ingredients

3 whites of egg   6oz castor sugar

Method: Have a thick board oiled and covered with oiled paper. Whisk the whites till very stiff, add a pinch of sugar, and whisk again till hard. Fold in all the sugar lightly. Put in a bag with a meringue pipe, and force out in fancy shapes on the paper. Dust with sugar, and put in a cool oven for several hours, till crisp throughout without browning. Remove from the paper, scoop out the inside, and dry off if necessary. Fill with whipped cream immediately before use, and decorate with pistachios.

Please note ~ meringue cases may be made in quantities, and kept in a tin.

Claret Pudding

Ingredients

Decoration - Wine jelly ½ pint claret
½ teacupful strawberry jam   1 lemon
Sugar to sweeten   ¼ glass brandy   ½oz gelatine
½ gill water   Dishing ~ a small jug of cream

Method: Line a border mould with wine jelly. Put all the ingredients into a saucepan, dissolve, and allow to infuse for twenty minutes. Strain, and allow to cool. Pour into the lined mould. Turn out when set, and fill the centre with whipped cream.

Silver Spark Jelly

Ingredients

1 pint liquid wine jelly 1 silver leaf

Put the silver leaf in a small basin with one tablespoonful jelly, break it up very small with a darning needle; add the rest of the jelly, and when just setting pour into a wetted mould. Turn out, and arrange chopped jelly round.

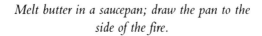

Melt butter in a saucepan; draw the pan to the side of the fire.

SAUCES & PASTRY

In pastry, lightness is the quality which is most to be desired; indeed, it is an essential. The manufacture of good pastry, requires a liberal allowance of "shortening" (butter, lard, or dripping). It is, moreover, also necessary to fold into, or entangle in the pastry, as much cold air as possible.

Anchovy Sauce

Ingredients

½oz butter   ½oz flour   ½ pint fish stock or milk
1 dessertspoonful anchovy essence pepper

Method: Melt butter in a saucepan; draw the pan to the side of the fire. Add the flour, and mix well with the back of a wooden spoon, then add about a third of the liquid, and stir carefully till boiling. Add the rest of the liquid gradually; bring to the boil and boil for three minutes. Season with pepper, and add the anchovy essence.

Horseradish Sauce

Ingredients

2 tablespoonfuls grated horseradish
1 gill cream   Salt and pepper
Good pinch of sugar, vinegar and lemon juice

Whip the cream fairly stiff and stir in the other ingredients.

Béchamel Sauce

Ingredients

¾oz butter   ¾oz flour   ½ pint milk
1 slice of carrot   1 small piece celery
½ small onion   1 blade of mace   2 cloves
6 white peppercorns, salt
1 tablespoonful cream

Method: Chop the vegetables and put in a pan with the milk, mace, peppercorns and cloves. Infuse in a warm place for half an hour, then strain. Melt the butter in a pan, add the flour and cook well without browning. Add the milk slowly and boil well. Pass through a tammy cloth, reheat, and add the cream.

Hollandaise Sauce

Ingredients

½ pint Béchamel sauce or melted butter sauce
2 yolks of egg   Lemon juice   Cayenne and salt

Method: Heat the sauce, stir in the yolks singly, and cook till they are thickened without boiling. Add the lemon juice and seasonings.

Velouté Sauce

Ingredients

1oz butter   ¾oz flour   ½ pint white stock
6 peppercorns   A few parsley stalks
4 chopped button mushrooms   Lemon juice
½ gill cream   Pepper and salt

Method: Fry the peppercorns, parsley stalks, and mushrooms in the butter without browning, stir in the flour, and add the stock. Simmer one hour, pass through a tammy cloth, and add the other ingredients.

Supreme Sauce

Ingredients

½ pint Velouté sauce 2 yolks of eggs ½oz butter
lemon juice 1 tablespoonful cream

Method: Heat the Velouté sauce; add the yolks and thicken them without boiling. Whisk in the butter in small pieces, and add the lemon juice and cream.

Brandy Sauce

Ingredients

1oz butter   ½oz flour   1½ gill water
½ gill brandy   ½oz sugar

Make a sauce with the butter, flour, and water. When cooked, add the sugar and brandy, and serve.

Chaud-Froid Sauce

Ingredients

½ pint Béchamel sauce   1 tablespoonful cream
1 gill stiff aspic jelly   Seasoning

Method: Mix together the sauce and the aspic jelly liquid when cool. Season the mixture, wring through a tammy cloth, and add the cream. Use when just beginning to thicken.
Please note ~ Brown or tomato sauce may be used instead of Béchamel sauce to vary the colour and flavour.

Shortcrust Pastry

Ingredients

½ lb flour   5oz butter   ½ teaspoonful salt
½ teaspoonful baking powder   1 yolk of egg
1 teaspoonful sugar   A little cold water

Method: Sieve the flour, salt and baking powder into a basin, and rub in the butter till fine. Add the sugar. Beat the yolk with a little water, and mix the pastry to a firm consistency. Knead lightly and roll as required.

Please note ~ for a plainer pastry, the yolk may be omitted and only 4oz shortening used. If for a savoury dish, omit the sugar.

Flaky Pastry

Ingredients

½ lb flour 6oz butter A little salt
Lemon juice Cold water

Method: Sieve the flour and salt into a basin, and mix to a firm paste with the lemon juice and cold water. Knead very thoroughly till smooth, and roll out thinly. Spread on one-third of the butter in small pats, sprinkle with a little flour, and fold the pastry in three. Turn the pastry half round, roll out, and repeat twice till the butter is all in. Roll and fold once more. Set aside if possible for half an hour before using it.

Please note ~ if the butter is very soft, the pastry may be set aside between the additions of butter.

The difference between puff and flaky pastry and short pastry is, that in the two former there are alternate thin layers of pastry and air, and in the latter there are small cavities all through the pastry caused by the expansion of the air.

𝒫uff Pastry

Ingredients
½ lb flour   ½ lb butter
½ teaspoonful lemon juice   Cold water

Method: Have the butter firm and dry in a floured cloth. Sieve the flour, and mix to a firm dough with the lemon juice and water, and knead very thoroughly. Roll out thinly, lay the butter in the centre and fold the pastry over it, roll and fold in three, and set aside for fifteen minutes in a cold place. Roll and fold it twice, and set aside again. Repeat this twice until the pastry has had seven rolls and seven folds. It is then ready to be rolled out for vol-au-vents, patties &c.

Please note ~ After each roll the pastry must be turned half round before being rolled again.

Choux Pastry

Ingredients

2oz flour   1oz butter   1 gill water   Pinch salt
Vanilla essence   1 egg and ½ yolk   1 gill cream

Method: Sieve the flour. Melt the butter, add the salt and water, and bring to the boil. Beat in the flour; cool, and add the eggs and vanilla essence. Place the mixture in small rolls on a greased tin; bake in a steady oven till brown and firm, about thirty minutes. When baked, scoop out the centre, and fill when cold with whipped and sweetened cream. Coat with glacé icing. If to be used with a savoury filling, omit the vanilla essence.

Weights and Measures for Cooks

Butter, soft (size of an egg) ... 1 oz

Butter 2 tea cups .... 1 lb

Flour 1 tablespoon(heaped) ... 1 oz

Sugar, brown 1 tablespoon .... 1 oz

Sugar, 2 tea cups (heaped) ..... 1 lb

4 teaspoons .... 1 tablespoon

25 grams .... 1 oz

450 grams .... 1 lb

54 English gallons .... 1 hogshead

English half pint .... 10 fl. oz

American half pint .... 8 fl oz

INCOME AND WAGES TABLE.

Per Year		Per Mth.		Per Wk.		Per Day.		Per Year.		Per Month.			Per Week		Per Day.	
£	s.	s.	d.	s.	d.	s.	d.	£	s.	£	s.	d.	s.	d.	s.	d.
1	0	1	8	0	4½	0	0¾	8	10	0	14	2	3	3¼	0	5½
1	10	2	6	0	7	0	1	9	0	0	15	0	3	5½	0	6
2	0	3	4	0	9	0	1¼	10	0	0	16	8	3	10¼	0	6½
2	10	4	2	0	11½	0	1¾	11	0	0	18	4	4	2¾	0	7¼
3	0	5	0	1	1¾	0	2	12	0	1	0	0	4	7½	0	8
3	10	5	10	1	4¼	0	2¼	13	0	1	1	8	5	0	0	8½
4	0	6	8	1	6½	0	2¾	14	0	1	3	4	5	4½	0	9¼
4	10	7	6	1	8¾	0	3	15	0	1	5	0	5	9¼	0	9¾
5	0	8	4	1	11	0	3¼	16	0	1	6	8	6	1¾	0	10½
5	10	9	2	2	1½	0	3¾	17	0	1	8	4	6	6½	0	11¼
6	0	10	0	2	3¾	0	4	18	0	1	10	0	6	11	0	11¾
6	10	10	10	2	6	0	4¼	19	0	1	11	8	7	3¾	1	0½
7	0	11	8	2	8¼	0	4½	20	0	1	13	4	7	8¼	1	1¼
7	10	12	6	2	10½	0	5	30	0	2	10	0	11	6½	1	7¾
8	0	13	4	3	1	0	5¼	40	0	3	6	8	15	4½	2	2¼

THE ETIQUETTE & RECIPES COLLECTIONS
A Copper Beech Book makes the perfect gift.

RECIPES FOR AN ENGLISH TEA
Recipes for the very best scones, preserves and cakes; recipes
for cleaning the silverware - even a recipe for
a spotless teapot!

RECIPES FOR ROSES
Make pot pourri, pomanders, perfumes and
sweet-smelling water.
Scented bags to lay with linen, scented gloves and
an excellent water for the head.

RECIPES FOR GARDENERS
Trusted hints and recipes - perfect for any keen gardener.

ETIQUETTE FOR CHOCOLATE LOVERS
Temptation through the years.
A special treat for all Chocolate Lovers.

For your free catalogue, write to

Copper Beech Publishing Ltd
P O Box 159 East Grinstead Sussex England RH19 4FS
www.copperbeechpublishing.co.uk